Cambridge English Readers

Level 4

Series editor: Philip Prowse

The Amsterdam Connection

Sue Leather

CAMBRIDGE
UNIVERSITY PRESS

PUBLISHED BY THE PRESS SYNDICATE OF THE UNIVERSITY OF CAMBRIDGE
The Pitt Building, Trumpington Street, Cambridge, United Kingdom

CAMBRIDGE UNIVERSITY PRESS
The Edinburgh Building, Cambridge CB2 2RU, UK
40 West 20th Street, New York, NY 10011-4211, USA
477 Williamstown Road, Port Melbourne VIC 3207, Australia
Ruiz de Alarcón 13, 28014 Madrid, Spain
Dock House, The Waterfront, Cape Town 8001, South Africa

http://www.cambridge.org

First published 2001
Fourth printing 2003

Printed in the United Kingdom at the University Press, Cambridge

Typeset in 12/15pt Adobe Garamond [CE]

ISBN 0 521 79502 8 (paperback)
ISBN 0 521 79503 6 (cassette)

Contents

Chapter 1	At the pub	6
Chapter 2	The past	10
Chapter 3	Amsterdam spring	15
Chapter 4	Talk with a striker	19
Chapter 5	Dinner at Sluizer's	26
Chapter 6	Bert's story	33
Chapter 7	Rotterdam	36
Chapter 8	Life gets interesting	41
Chapter 9	The Amsterdam Connection	46
Chapter 10	A policeman	50
Chapter 11	A football match	53
Chapter 12	A goalkeeper	57
Chapter 13	A plan	61
Chapter 14	Prisoner	64
Chapter 15	Stories	71
Chapter 16	Goodbye Amsterdam	76

Characters

Kate Jensen: a news reporter on the *Daily Echo* in London
Rick: Kate's friend, also a news reporter
Dave Balzano: the editor of the *Daily Echo*
Elly van Praage: a policewoman in the Amsterdam police and Kate's friend
Max Carson: Kate's friend and ex-boss
Tom Carson: Max's brother, owner of Rotterdam City Football Club
Martijn Christiaans: a Dutch businessman
Jos van Essen: a retired footballer
Raúl Sanchez: goalkeeper at Rotterdam City Football Club
Joop de Vries: an inspector in the Amsterdam police
Bert: a criminal

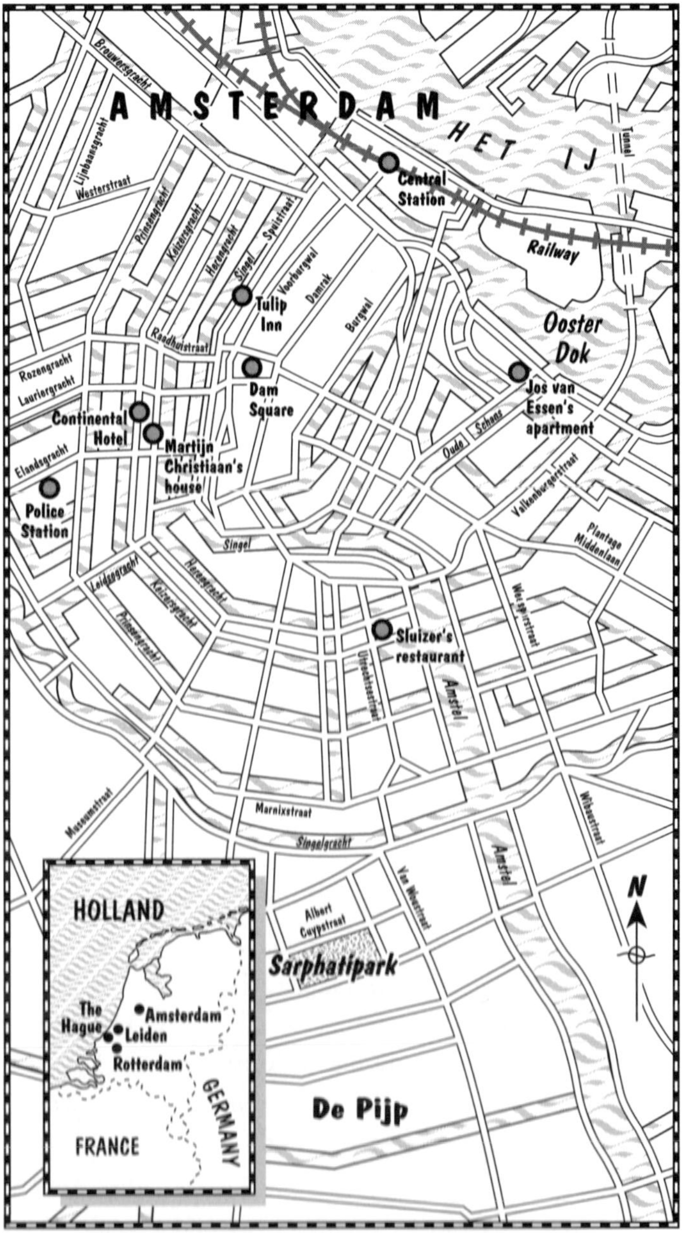
AMSTERDAM
HET IJ
Central Station
Railway
Tunnel
Ooster Dok
Jos van Essen's apartment
Tulip Inn
Dam Square
Continental Hotel
Martijn Christiaan's house
Police Station
Sluizer's restaurant
Brouwersgracht
Lijnbaansgracht
Westerstraat
Prinsengracht
Keizersgracht
Herengracht
Singel
Spuistraat
Voorburgwal
Damrak
Burgwal
Raadhuisstraat
Rozengracht
Lauriergracht
Elandsgracht
Oude Schans
Valkenburgerstraat
Plantage Middenlaan
Leidsegracht
Weesperstraat
Utrechtsestraat
Amstel
Marnixstraat
Singelgracht
Museumstraat
Wibautstraat
Van Woustraat
Albert Cuypstraat
Sarphatipark
De Pijp
N
HOLLAND
The Hague
Amsterdam
Leiden
Rotterdam
GERMANY
FRANCE

Chapter 1 *At the pub*

'You need a holiday, Kate,' said Max Carson. It was early evening and we were having a beer in the Queen's Head. 'A break from London,' he added.

'Oh sure, Max.' I smiled. 'Go and tell Balzano. I'm sure he'll agree with you!'

Dave Balzano was an excellent newspaper editor, but he was often angry with his reporters. In fact, he was famous for his bad temper. The thought of Balzano giving me a holiday because I needed one was funny. I said this to Max.

'So Dave hasn't changed, then?' asked Max, laughing. Max knew Dave – and me – from some years ago when we all worked on the *Manchester Evening News*. Max was the editor and Dave was head of foreign news. Max gave me my first job. I was just a young reporter then, trying to make a name for myself. That was before I came to London.

'Er ... no,' I said. 'He certainly hasn't.' I smiled and drank some of my beer. 'But tell me about you,' I added.

I hadn't seen much of Max for a while, mainly because he lived in Holland now. He had been born there. His mother was Dutch, his father was English. He came to England when he was in his early twenties to train as a journalist and he stayed. But Max retired from the *Evening News* five years ago when he was fifty-five, and returned to Holland.

'I'm fine,' said Max.

'And the club?' I asked.

Max's brother, Tom, was the owner and manager of Rotterdam City Football Club and the Carson Football School. When Max left the *Manchester Evening News* he had joined his brother, to help him with his business. Max now had about twenty-five per cent of the shares and a nice income for his 'retirement'.

'It's OK,' said Max.

'Only OK?' I asked, surprised.

'Mmm ... yes,' said Max. I got the feeling that he didn't really want to talk about it, so we changed the subject.

Max didn't often come to England these days, except to see friends and to look for new players for Rotterdam City Football Club. When he did come to London he would come to the *Echo*'s offices to see me and we usually had a beer at the Queen's Head. It was a typical central London pub, full of office workers with mobile phones. It was smoky and noisy at this time in the evening, but the beer was good.

'So what's happening here in London, Kate?' Max asked.

Max always asked me about my latest story; he liked to know what was happening. He still loved the newspaper business. He and Balzano were complete opposites, and not just because Balzano's father was Italian and Max's mother was Dutch. Balzano was a very good editor, but you never knew when he was going to explode. Max, though, was calm and easy to work with – he was one of the best.

I told him about my last story and the reason I was so exhausted.

'You just need a break,' Max said again.

Max was right, I did need a holiday. Life in the city had been really tough for the past few months. I had had some difficult murder stories, the usual zero information from the London police and Balzano pushing me as usual. I was beginning to feel tired and the idea of getting away from London was a very attractive one.

'You like Holland, don't you?' asked Max suddenly.

I laughed. 'Well, yes, but ... ' I'd been to Amsterdam once, chasing a story, and I'd loved it.

'And you know something about sport,' he added.

'Well, I know about karate and a bit about boxing,' I said. 'I don't know that much about other sports.' I had trained in karate for ten years and my father had been a boxer when he was young.

I looked at Max, waiting for the rest.

'Listen,' he said, 'why don't you come and write a story about our club in Holland?'

Rotterdam City Football Club was one of the top clubs in Europe now. Many of the young men who had been trained at the school – the Carson Football School – played for Rotterdam City. The club took kids who could play football off the streets and trained them to be the best. Football schools like theirs were one reason why Holland had so many great footballers. It was perfect: the school and the club.

Max had always been crazy about football. When he was editor of the *Evening News* he spent all his free time watching football matches. He even took me to see Manchester United once. He was one of those guys who knew the name of every footballer in Europe.

'What me?' I laughed. 'A sports reporter? You know me, Max, I only write about crime.'

Max smiled. 'I know, Kate, and you're great. But it would be a holiday for you!'

Max looked at his watch and finished his beer quickly. He had arranged to have dinner with a friend that evening and he had to leave immediately. He was already late. He got up, promising that he would ring me in a few days.

But Max never rang. In fact, I never saw him again. Two days later, he was found lying dead in an Amsterdam street with twenty knife wounds in his body.

Chapter 2 *The past*

'Why did it happen, Rick?' I asked my colleague over and over again. 'It makes no sense. No sense at all.'

Rick and I were both news reporters on the *Daily Echo*. Our desks sat side by side. We worked together every day and at times like this Rick was the person I usually talked to. We'd heard the news of Max's death from the police in London.

'It was probably just a mugger, Kate, trying to get Max's money,' said Rick gently.

'What, in Amsterdam?' I said.

Amsterdam is one of the safest cities in the world. Soft drugs and sex, yes, but not much crime at all, certainly not violent crime. I had got to know the city quite well about two years before during a story about a British guy who was selling stolen paintings there. At that time I'd made a friend in the Dutch police.

Max had been found by the police in an area of Amsterdam called de Pijp in the early hours of the morning. I knew the Dutch police thought it was a mugging that had gone wrong – a drunk or a drug addict who tried to steal Max's money. It looked as if Max had fought back, but unfortunately the guy had a knife and had gone crazy.

'But what was Max doing walking around in the middle of the night?' I asked. 'And in Amsterdam – he didn't live in Amsterdam.'

Rick turned away from his computer screen and looked me straight in the eyes.

'Well, you know, Kate ... men in Amsterdam ... ' he started. He didn't have to continue.

Amsterdam is the sex capital of Europe; everyone knows that. But I couldn't imagine Max visiting the famous red-light district of Amsterdam. I didn't know why exactly, but somehow it just wasn't like him. Not the Max I knew.

'Max?' I said. 'I don't think so.'

I had to admit that Rick was right, though. Max could have been there for any reason. After all, he lived in Holland. And why should Max tell me what he was planning to do? It wasn't as if we saw each other that often. I wondered now if I had really known him at all.

I thought for a moment and then said, 'You know, Rick, there's something I've never told you about Max.'

'What's that?' asked Rick.

'He saved my life,' I said.

'Saved your life?' repeated Rick, turning round to give me his full attention.

'Yes,' I said. 'When I first started as a reporter on the *Manchester Evening News* they asked me to write stories about babies and marriages. You know, the usual sort of thing ... '

Rick smiled and nodded. He knew exactly what I meant. His first job had been in a small town in Scotland where he spent two years writing about sheep stealing.

'But I really wanted to write about crime,' I continued. 'You know ... I was really young and really stupid, I guess. I wanted to write a big story – the biggest. I was hoping to make a name for myself by catching a really big fish.'

'Well, that's natural,' said Rick.

'Yeah, the problem was that the big fish was Johnny McGraw, one of Manchester's most dangerous criminals. He was really bad news, the kind of guy who would put people in the river with weights tied around their feet.'

'So what happened?' asked Rick.

'Max gave me this easy story, a break-in at a house in the centre of Manchester. The guy who lived in the house had tried to stop the gang from stealing his things. There was a fight and the man died of his wounds, so it became a murder. There were witnesses, people who saw it happen, but nobody could make them talk about it. Not even the police.'

I took a drink of my coffee. 'Anyway,' I continued, 'the guys were part of Johnny McGraw's gang and McGraw would kill anyone who talked.'

'And you tried to get them to talk?' asked Rick.

'You guessed it,' I said. 'It was my chance to get a really big story! But Johnny McGraw knew that it would lead back to him. He put a contract on my head for £25,000. If anyone killed me, McGraw would give them that amount of money.'

'So then what happened?' asked Rick, his eyes wide.

'Well, you can imagine that a lot of people were trying to kill me. I had to have police protection for a while,' I said. 'My own policemen twenty-four hours a day. I mean it was really serious. Then time went by and nothing happened. After about a month I came out of hiding and everything seemed fine. But then McGraw's men caught me.'

'But you got free?' Rick asked.

'Yes, with Max's help. Max knew where I was going that evening. When I disappeared he went out to look for me. He put his own life in danger for me. Finally, he came to an arrangement with McGraw and McGraw let me go,' I said.

I stopped. I wanted to cry but I couldn't.

'Anyway,' I continued, 'Max saved my life and I've never forgotten it.'

'Wow, Kate . . . that's quite a story,' said Rick.

'Yeah,' I said. 'I've never told you, I guess because I was just so stupid. I hate to talk about how stupid I was,' I said.

Rick touched my arm and smiled.

But that was all in the past and now Max was dead. There were a number of people at the *Echo* who knew Max, and they all found his death hard to believe: it was so sudden and violent. For me the whole thing was worse because I'd seen him so recently. I knew that I had to go to Amsterdam, and I knew that if I wanted to go I had to ask my editor, Dave Balzano.

* * *

'You want to go where, Jensen?' shouted Balzano. He was a fat sweaty man and he never spoke quietly.

'Amsterdam,' I said.

'Why do you want to do that?' asked Balzano angrily. 'Max was killed by a drug addict who was trying to get money!' Then he stopped for a moment. I could see that Balzano was sad at Max's death. After all, Max had been his editor too.

I looked at Balzano. 'I want to go, Dave,' I said quietly.

Balzano knew Max was special to me. He knew what had happened back in Manchester.

'OK, OK,' he said finally. 'Why don't you take Rick with you?'

'No, there's no need ... really,' I said. I wasn't sure what I would find out, if anything, but I knew I had to go. And I had to go alone. I caught the first plane I could. I was going to Amsterdam as Max had wanted – not to write about his club, but to find his killer.

Chapter 3 *Amsterdam spring*

I arrived in Amsterdam at 9.30 on Monday morning. I rang Elly van Praag of the Dutch police from Schiphol airport. Elly was the friend I had made during the case of the stolen paintings two years ago.

Elly wasn't working that morning and we arranged to meet two hours later at a café we knew in the Jordaan, an old part of Amsterdam. That would give me time to go to my hotel and check in. I caught the train from the airport and took a taxi into the centre from Central Station. The *Echo* had booked me into a hotel on the Keizersgracht. There were a lot of visitors to Amsterdam in spring and good rooms were difficult to find. The hotel wasn't very nice, but I didn't expect to be staying long. I left my bag and went to meet Elly.

Elly was already at the café when I arrived, sitting at a table outside, next to the Prinsengracht canal. She smiled and stood up as she saw me coming, and kissed me three times in the Dutch way. 'Hey, Kate, wonderful to see you,' she said.

Elly was typically Dutch, if there is such a thing. She was tall and very blonde, and looked like a sportswoman. In fact, she was a very good cyclist, and when she wasn't fighting crime in Amsterdam, was usually to be found cycling hundreds of kilometres around Holland with a number on her back. She looked like the daughter of a Dutch farmer, which she was, with red cheeks and bright blue eyes. And like most Dutch people of her age – she was in her early thirties – she spoke English very well.

We sat down and ordered coffee. It was a fine spring day; the sky was blue with little white clouds here and there.

'I'm sorry about your friend,' Elly said.

'Yes,' I said, staring at the red and white tablecloth. 'It's really sad.'

I told her about my meeting with Max just a few days ago. 'He seemed to be happy and said the club was doing OK,' I added.

Elly wasn't a football fan and knew nothing about the Rotterdam club. She did know about crime in Amsterdam though.

De Pijp, where Max had died, was one of the oldest parts of the city, a lively place with a wonderful street market at its centre, on a street called Albert Cuypstraat. Last time I was in Amsterdam I had gone shopping there for Dutch cheese and tulips to take home. It was strange to think that this lovely colourful place was where Max had lost his life.

'De Pijp is getting quite dangerous these days, Kate,' Elly said. 'There have been quite a number of stabbings and shootings. We've been busy down there.'

'So, it just looks like it was a mugging that went wrong?' I asked.

The waiter arrived with the coffees, Elly's black and mine *koffie verkeerd* or 'wrong coffee', the Dutch name for coffee with milk. Elly had ordered a cake too. All that crime-fighting and cycling made her hungry.

'Mmm,' said Elly, drinking some of her strong black

coffee. 'I'm afraid that's what it looks like, Kate. He was just in the wrong place at the wrong time. Poor guy,' she added. 'Of course, there will have to be a postmortem.'

The police always asked for the examination of a body found like this. I thought of Max lying dead with twenty knife wounds in his body. I felt cold, although the spring air was warm.

'So who found him?' I asked.

'We did. Well, one of the police teams going round the city late Thursday night,' Elly replied.

Thursday. Just two days after I had met Max at the Queen's Head. I looked out over the canal. It was a lovely warm day and the streets and bridges over the canals were full of people on bikes or on foot. It was beautiful. It was hard to think that Max was dead, and even harder to imagine that he had died in Amsterdam. It was such a lovely city.

'He was staying at the Tulip Inn on Spuistraat,' said Elly.

I didn't know the hotel, but I knew that Spuistraat was right in the old centre of the city.

'They didn't find much on his body at all. Just the usual,' she said.

Just the usual. In death people were almost the same. Some money perhaps, a few business cards, perhaps some photographs of the family. Except Max didn't have much family: his wife had died years ago and they didn't have any children. There was just his brother, Tom.

'Did the killer take his money, then?' I asked. If it was a mugging, surely the only reason could be money.

'Well, the police couldn't find his wallet,' she said.

Of course, that meant nothing, I thought. If someone

wanted to make it look like a mugging, the first thing they would do was take money.

'We think that he probably fought back and his attacker went mad. It happens,' said Elly.

It certainly did.

'Why did he stay the night?' I asked. 'Why didn't he just go back to The Hague? It's only forty minutes or so on the train.'

I knew that Max lived near The Hague. He had asked me to stay at his house a few times, although I never had. I never seemed to have time. Now I would never have the chance.

'He must have had a business meeting the next morning. Apparently he often stayed in Amsterdam,' Elly said. 'The hotel manager said he'd stayed at that hotel before.'

Elly got up to go to work.

'Who's in charge of Max's case?' I asked.

'Joop de Vries, Murder Squad' she said. Her face told me that she didn't like him much. 'Oh yes,' she added as she unlocked her bike and got on it. 'There was a card with a name and address in Max's pocket. I took a note of it.' She put her hand in her jacket pocket and brought out a piece of paper with something written on it. She gave it to me. It said: 'Jos van Essen, Oude Schans 141.'

I didn't know much about football, but I knew that name. Jos van Essen was one of the greatest footballers of all time.

Chapter 4 *Talk with a striker*

I watched Elly cycle off over the bridge, her blue jacket blowing out behind her.

I sat back down at the table and thought. Jos van Essen was a great footballer, like Pelé, Cruyff or Shearer. A real star. He had played for Holland lots of times as a striker and always scored lots of goals. He was also very good-looking. There were always reports in the newspapers about his girlfriends, who were usually models or actresses. I remembered that I'd recently read in the newspaper that he'd retired from football. People had been surprised because he was only twenty-eight, still quite young to retire.

I took out my map. Oude Schans was a long walk away. I had been there last time I was in Amsterdam, when I went to the Bimhuis jazz club. It was a very nice part of the city. It was a lovely day so I decided to walk, and do some thinking as I went. I walked off towards Oude Schans to see the ex-footballer.

There was a light wind and a smell of salt as I crossed the canal. The sea was never far away in Amsterdam. I turned onto Raadhuistraat and walked towards Dam Square. So it looked as if Max had come to Amsterdam on business. I felt happy that Rick had been wrong about him coming for sex. That would mean that Max had been lonely and I didn't want to think of him as a lonely old man.

The retired footballer lived in an apartment beside the canal, Oude Schans, in one of the oldest parts of

Amsterdam. It was 1.30 when I got to his apartment block. I pressed the bell and Jos van Essen's voice came through the intercom. I told him I was a friend of Max's and the door opened.

'Come up to the top floor, Miss Jensen,' he said. His voice was soft and pleasant.

Like all Dutch houses, this one was tall and thin, and the stairs were very narrow. I finally got to the top and knocked. I heard the sound of van Essen unlocking his door. It took some time – there were three or four locks. Then there he was, smiling. He had a beautiful smile.

'It's quite a climb, isn't it?' he said. He looked just like the pictures I'd seen of him on the *Echo*'s sports pages. He was tall, with the most beautiful dark brown eyes and the whitest teeth I'd ever seen. He was wearing black jeans and a pink shirt, which looked great against his black skin. His body still looked fit. And what a body! I was beginning to like my work.

'Come in, Miss Jensen,' he said, still smiling. He held open the door and showed me into his apartment.

The apartment was not very big, but apartments in Holland are usually quite small. He must have been very rich, though – the furniture looked expensive. I remembered reading something in a newspaper about him when he was still playing for Rotterdam. The newspaper story had said that he was earning millions. I supposed that this was just his city apartment. He would have a big house somewhere, perhaps at the beach. Perhaps abroad.

Although the apartment was small, it was in a great position. It looked right onto the canal, and the house where Rembrandt had lived was nearby. The large French windows were open and I could feel the warm air coming into the room. The only sign that the apartment was owned by a footballer was the photograph on the coffee table of the Rotterdam City team which had won the European Cup four years ago. Jos was in the front row. Max and a man who looked like him but younger – Tom I guessed – were standing beside the team smiling.

'Ah, yes, the good times!' he said, seeing me look at the photo. 'When we were the best!' Jos looked a little sad.

He offered me a comfortable armchair, then said, 'Have some coffee, Miss Jensen. I have a fresh pot ready.' He went into the kitchen and returned almost immediately with the coffee.

'So, you're a sports reporter, writing about Rotterdam City?' he asked as he put the coffee pot on the low glass table.

'Yes, I'd like to write about the club,' I said. 'I think football fans in England would find it interesting.'

I explained that I'd seen Max just two days before he died.

'You're a friend of Max's?' he said, pouring me a cup of coffee. 'It's just so sad, awful ... What a terrible thing to happen. I can hardly believe it.'

Jos van Essen looked like he was going to cry, but he managed to stop himself.

'Yes, it's terrible,' I said, 'and so senseless. The police think he was killed by a mugger.'

'Yes,' said Jos in a worried voice. 'That's what they think ... '

For a moment I thought that he was going to say more, but he decided not to.

'You knew Max well then?' I continued.

'Oh yes, I knew him very well. He really helped me when he came to the club. Really helped me to become a great footballer.'

He reached for his coffee cup. Again I thought he was trying not to cry. Then he went on.

'Rotterdam City Football Club was good to me,' he said, looking at the photo again. 'I was a ten-year-old kid in a children's home when Tom Carson found me. You know the story, it's famous. Tom came along and watched me play. He saw something, something that no-one else could see. He took me to the Carson School, gave me a good education, fed me, let me play football. At the school they trained me how to really play ... They gave me football boots for the first time.'

He smiled. 'I still have my first pair of football boots,' he continued. 'Before that I'd only played in old trainers. They gave me the opportunity to be really good. And for the first time in my life I was happy.'

Jos looked at me and took a deep breath.

'And then Max really helped me to be the best,' he said. 'When he came to the club I was a good footballer. But Max talked to me, helped me, gave me what I needed to play for Holland, to become great ... and he was great, a great man.'

Jos van Essen had played for Holland and had been in the team that had won the World Cup.

'I don't really understand what Max's job was at the club,' I said. 'Isn't Tom the coach, the manager?'

'Yes, that's right,' said Jos. 'Max was a scout. He helped Tom by travelling around Holland and the rest of Europe, looking for good young players for the club and kids for the school.'

'And it seems he was good at it,' I said.

'The best,' said Jos.

Max had always been very active and even after he'd retired, he still loved to travel and to work. I also remembered that Max had always known when a young football player was going to be great.

'Were Max and his brother close? Did they have a good relationship?' I asked.

Jos looked a little uncomfortable. 'Yes … ' he answered slowly. 'Although they've been arguing lately.'

'What about?'

'I don't know,' Jos said and looked away. I had a feeling he knew more than he would say.

'Why did Max have your card on him when he was found?' I asked. If Jos and Max knew each other so well, why did he need a visiting card?

'I've just moved here. It's my new apartment,' explained van Essen, smiling and waving his hand around the room. 'I saw Max on Thursday evening and gave him my new address, that's all.'

'You saw him on Thursday?' I asked.

That was the evening Max was found dead in de Pijp.

'Yes,' he said. 'I told the police. Thursday evening, early, about seven. We had a drink together at De Beiaard bar on Herengracht. We often met there when we were both in town, just for a chat and a beer.' He smiled and added, 'They have a great choice of beer.'

'And then?' I asked.

'I don't know what he did exactly,' said Jos. 'I had a dinner date and he said he had to visit someone.'

'Did he say who?' I asked.

'No.'

'Was he walking?' I asked.

'No. He said he was going to get a taxi,' Jos answered.

'So, the person he was visiting didn't live in the centre,' I said.

'I'm not sure,' said Jos. 'Max often took taxis even short distances. He didn't like to get too tired because of his heart.'

'His heart?' I asked.

'Yeah, Max had a bad heart. He had a heart attack … oh, about four years ago I think,' said Jos.

That was something I didn't know about Max.

'And he took pills?'

'Yeah, I think so … Yes, I'm sure. I've seen him take them quite a few times,' Jos replied.

'Max told me that there were some problems at the club,' I lied.

Jos looked surprised.

'Er … well, yes. I don't know. I don't really know anything about it. I left about a year ago,' he said. 'I don't know what's going on now.' He looked away from me.

'You didn't talk about it?' I asked.

'No, we didn't,' said Jos. He said it in a way that made it sound like there was nothing more to say.

'And what about your retirement from football? Why are you retiring at only twenty-eight?' I asked. 'It's very young.'

'Oh, you know, I want to do other things,' he said, still

looking away. 'I'm not sure what yet, but something different. I'm still young but I've been playing football for a long time, Miss Jensen.'

I drank my coffee and got up to go.

'I'm staying at the Continental on Keizersgracht,' I said as I was leaving.

Jos van Essen unlocked the four locks on his door and said goodbye.

Chapter 5 *Dinner at Sluizer's*

An hour after ringing van Essen's doorbell I was back on Oude Schans, looking at the boats on the canal and watching the light dancing on the water.

I looked at my map and wondered what to do. Perhaps I'd go to de Pijp, the area of the city where Max's body had been found.

De Pijp was at the other end of Amsterdam so I walked a little in the warm sunshine, then took the tram. When I got there I walked around the streets for a while and through the market. It was an interesting colourful place. You could buy anything there: fresh fruit and vegetables, meat, eggs, cheese and flowers. Holland was famous for its tulips of course, and the tulips here were lovely.

I passed by the narrow street where Elly told me they had found Max. At one end of it was a bigger street; at the other end was a park called Sarphatipark. It was this area around the park that was becoming more and more dangerous, Elly had said. There was only one apartment block on one side of the street. Even in the sunshine, it looked sad and grey.

The police had put a rope around the area where Max had died to stop people going near it. I felt cold as I looked at it. I went into a small café-bar on one corner of the market, sat at the bar and ordered tea to warm myself up.

There were only a few customers in the bar, mostly men who looked like they worked on the market. The bar owner was a friendly guy with a big stomach and a red face. He started talking to me. His English was quite good. We chatted about this and that, and then I said, 'I heard there was a murder here the other night.'

'Oh yes,' said the barman. 'Big trouble. We've had the police here almost all the time.'

'Does it happen a lot around here?' I asked.

'Well, it's getting worse,' he said.

'It's terrible what's happening to this area,' said a voice at my side.

I turned round. Next to me was an old guy drinking jenever, the strong Dutch gin, and smoking a cigarette. He was short and his skin was dark, like he had worked outside all of his life. He had very little hair and when he smiled at me I noticed that he had just a few dark brown teeth.

'I'm Bert,' he said, holding out his hand.

Bert liked to talk. He asked me where I was from and we talked about London, which he had visited twenty years before. We chatted for a while, then returned to the murder.

'Everybody round here heard about it,' he said. 'It happened just two streets away.' He took a drink of his jenever. 'Yes, the place was full of police for days.' Bert's face looked sad. 'It's terrible … terrible.' I wondered whether it was the violent crime or having the police around so much in de Pijp that Bert thought was so terrible.

We talked some more as I drank my tea and then I got up to go. 'If you hear anything about what happened, give me a call. I'm a friend of the dead guy's family,' I lied. I gave Bert a piece of paper with the telephone number and the name of my hotel. He was staring at the paper as I left the bar.

I went back to the hotel. In my room I lay down on the bed. I had a few questions in my head: Why had Max wanted me to write about the club so much? Was it just that he thought I needed a holiday? And why was Jos van Essen so frightened? I put a John Coltrane cassette in my walkman and listened to some of the best jazz saxophone music the world has ever known.

I woke up to the sound of the phone on my bedside table ringing in my ears. It took me a second to realise that I'd been asleep, another to remember where I was. I still had my headphones on my ears, although the cassette had stopped. I shook myself awake and took the headphones off. It was Elly.

'Uh ... Elly, what's up?' I was still stupid with sleep and had no idea what time it was. It was dark, though.

'Kate, are you asleep?' she asked.

'Well, I was. What time is it?' I asked, waking up a little.

'It's seven o'clock and I've just finished work. Kate, let's meet for a drink,' she said.

Half an hour later we were in a bar near the hotel having a beer. I told Elly about my meeting with van Essen and my visit to de Pijp.

'You're lucky!' she said and smiled. 'Most women would kill for the chance of talking to van Essen.'

'Well, most of the time I'm interviewing ugly criminals.' I laughed. 'It was great to have someone attractive to talk to!'

'Did you get anything interesting?' she asked.

'Not much,' I said. 'But I got the feeling that he's frightened of something … or somebody. His apartment was locked up like a bank!'

Elly laughed.

'I'm just going to ring Balzano,' I said, moving towards the telephone at the other end of the bar. I didn't have much to tell him, but it was always a good idea to keep him calm.

'No, wait,' she said and held onto my arm. 'Wait until after dinner. I've got something to tell you.'

We chose Sluizer's restaurant on Utrechtsestraat for dinner and took a taxi there. It was one of my favourite Amsterdam restaurants. It was really two restaurants, the fish restaurant and the meat restaurant, and they were both wonderful. There were beautiful old mirrors everywhere and waiters in black suits and white aprons. And the food was always great; it didn't matter which part you chose. Tonight we chose the meat restaurant. We sat down and ordered steaks and a bottle of Bordeaux. It had been a busy day and I was very hungry.

Suddenly Elly looked at me in that special way she did when she had something important to say. I could see her serious face in the large mirror next to the table. 'Kate, there's something I need to tell you,' she said.

'Mmm?' I said, chewing a piece of steak.

'They think they found Max's killer today,' she said.

I put my knife and fork down. 'They?' I asked.

'De Vries's men. They picked someone up. They're fairly sure he did it.'

'But has this guy confessed – said that he did it?' I asked.

'No,' she said. 'I don't think so, but they found Max's

wallet in his apartment. They're looking for the knife now.'

'Who is it?' I asked.

'A guy who lives in the area,' she said. 'A well-known local drug addict and mugger.'

So that was it, I thought. It looked like everyone was right. Max's murder had been a senseless killing by a sick guy who needed money for drugs. I put my head in my hands – I felt ill.

'I'm sorry, Kate,' Elly added.

I couldn't speak for a moment. Then, suddenly, the memory of Max talking to me at the Queen's Head that night came back to me. 'You need a holiday,' he had said. 'Come and write about the club.' Why exactly did Max want me to write about Rotterdam City?

'I don't believe it,' I said, looking up. The words were a surprise, even to me.

I guessed that the Amsterdam police wanted to catch the killer quickly. And it would be easier for them if the killer was a local criminal who was annoying them. They were just like police everywhere.

'But Kate . . . ' started Elly.

'I don't know why, but there's something about this that isn't right,' I almost shouted. The middle-aged couple sitting near us looked towards me. I was sweating, and I still felt sick. I spoke more quietly. 'There's something else . . . '

Elly smiled kindly at me. 'Look, Kate, I'm just telling you. I'm not even working on the murder.' I knew that was true. Elly was working on another crime on the other side of the city.

'I know, Elly, and thanks,' I said. 'But I just have a feeling . . . '

She smiled again. 'I don't know what the truth is,' she continued, 'but I thought I'd better tell you. Tomorrow de Vries will tell the newspapers and TV and everyone in the world will know.'

I knew that Elly thought that my feelings for Max were so strong that I couldn't accept his death, couldn't accept the way that he had died. I was beginning to wonder about it myself. It was hard when a guy had saved your life. It was hard to see things clearly. I wondered what Balzano would think.

Balzano! I suddenly remembered I had to phone him. I quickly drank half a glass of wine to make me brave, and ran to the phone in the hall.

'Jensen!' screamed Balzano. I held the phone away from my ear for a moment. Balzano was unhappy about something and when he was unhappy he never said hello.

'At last! I thought you'd disappeared,' he shouted. Disappeared! I'd only been in Amsterdam one day.

'Listen,' he continued, 'there's a story in the *Gazette* this evening about Max. By Joe Simmons.' Balzano said the name through his teeth. The *Gazette* was the other big newspaper in London, and Joe Simmons was their best reporter.

'What . . . what's Simmons saying?' I asked.

'That they've found the guy who killed Max,' Balzano continued. 'That it's all over. What the hell are you doing there, running round Amsterdam . . . What am I paying you for, Jensen?'

Even with the phone held away from my ear I could hear Balzano clearly.

This was bad news. Simmons had somehow got the story first, and one thing that made Balzano really angry was when the *Gazette* got a story before us. Well, I wasn't happy about it either.

Balzano stopped for a few seconds to catch his breath and I jumped in.

'Dave, listen. It's not true . . . at least I don't think it is,' I said, hoping I was right.

'Not true?' screamed Balzano. 'For God's sake, Jensen. They've found Max's wallet! The guy had his wallet! What more do you want?'

'I don't know Dave,' I said. 'I just have a feeling that there's something else. Give me time.'

I put the phone down.

'Well?' asked Elly, who had almost finished her steak by the time I returned. All that cycling certainly made her hungry.

'Bad news,' I said. 'The news is out already, true or not, and Balzano is not a happy man. He nearly had a heart attack when I said I needed time, but he agreed in the end.' Elly laughed. She had never met Balzano, but she understood.

Balzano had given me three days to find a story or leave Amsterdam. I pulled my steak, now getting cold, back towards me. I had a feeling that I was going to need all my strength.

Chapter 6 *Bert's story*

Back at the hotel there was a message from Bert, the old guy I'd met in the bar in de Pijp. He'd left a telephone number. It was late but I rang him from my room. Bert was still at the bar where I'd left him hours before – I could hear people talking behind him and the sound of glasses. I wondered if he spent all his time there.

'I have some information for you,' he said. 'Some really good information. But I need something.'

'Something?' I asked.

'Some money,' he whispered. 'Four hundred guilders.' Four hundred guilders. That was over a hundred pounds. It was lot of money if the information was useless, but I had to say yes. Balzano was getting very impatient and I had nothing else.

'OK, Bert, that's fine,' I said. 'Can you come to the hotel now?'

Bert arrived at the hotel at 11.30, looking a lot more drunk than when I had left him. We went into the bar; he ordered jenever and I paid for it. I had put the four hundred guilders in an envelope and now I put it on the table, my hand covering it.

'Well, Bert,' I said. 'What is it?'

He looked around the room, as if he were expecting someone to be listening. Then he looked at the envelope and drank some of his jenever.

'I know someone,' he whispered. 'He saw what happened to your friend on Wednesday night. Says your friend was already dead when he was taken to that street. Someone took him out of a car, then knifed him many times. But he was already dead. He was dead before. He's sure of it.'

Bert looked at the envelope under my hand. I didn't move it. 'Why doesn't this person talk to the police?' I asked.

Bert laughed. 'Oh, he doesn't like the police, you know. He won't tell the police anything!' Well, that was possible. There were a lot of people who didn't like the police. Especially if they were criminals.

'And where was he, this person?' I asked.

'He was looking from an upstairs window,' said Bert. 'Something woke him up. He didn't turn the light on, just went to the window. He could see everything.'

I wondered whether Bert was telling the truth. It was more likely, I guessed, that this person was breaking into a house at the time and that was why he couldn't tell the police. I imagined that Bert had friends like that. Or was it even Bert himself?

'Was it a man or a woman with my friend?' I asked.

'Well, a man, my friend guesses, but it was dark,' said Bert.

'And the car, what kind of car was it?' I asked.

Bert thought. He didn't know. It was too dark and anyway it was parked down the other end of the street.

'I thought he could see everything,' I said.

'Well, you know, almost everything,' said Bert. 'He saw someone stabbing him with a knife, that's certain.'

'So what about the knife?' I asked. 'What happened to it?'

Bert just shook his head. 'Who knows?' he said.

'Look, Bert,' I said. 'I know the police have already picked up a guy. They say they found my friend's wallet in his apartment.'

'I know, I know,' said Bert impatiently. 'But it's not true. The guy they picked up – Cor Schaap – he couldn't kill anyone, everyone on the street knows that. He's never killed anyone before. Why should he start now?'

'There's always a first time,' I said.

'No, no,' said Bert. 'He just stole the wallet from the dead body. That's what everyone thinks ... Everyone except the police.'

Well, I thought, it was possible.

I gave Bert the envelope. He took it quickly, finished his drink and almost ran out of the door with the money. I had no idea whether the information he'd given me was true. Perhaps Bert had just seen the opportunity to make some easy money. It could be an expensive hundred pounds for me.

I went back to my room, lay on my bed, and looked at a report of Rotterdam Football Club's match against Leiden last night. It was from *Het Parool*, a Dutch newspaper. I couldn't read Dutch but I could see that Rotterdam had lost 2–0 to Leiden. Rotterdam had played very badly.

I wondered what Tom Carson, Manager of Rotterdam City FC, would have to say about that.

Chapter 7 *Rotterdam*

Amsterdam Central Station is a beautiful building, but I didn't have much time to look at it. My meeting with Tom Carson was at 10.00 on Tuesday morning at the Rotterdam City Football Club offices. It was almost 8.30 when I arrived at the station and bought a ticket, some coffee and a croissant, and got on the train.

Holland is such a small country that all the towns and cities are close to each other. It would take me just over an hour to get to Rotterdam, so I sat back in my seat and enjoyed the view. Flat green fields, flower farms and cows. And of course, water. In Holland there is water everywhere.

It was hard not to think about Max's death. Before leaving me the night before, Elly had warned me not to get too involved. But I was involved already. I had become involved when Max Carson had talked to me just a few days ago in the Queen's Head. I was involved because Max was dead. I was involved because he had saved my life: I owed him something.

As I looked out of the window at the Dutch countryside, I thought about what I'd read last night about Rotterdam's match against Leiden. I didn't know much about football, but I knew you had to score goals to win. Tom Carson would not be happy, I guessed. But there were more important things than football – the guy had just lost his brother.

The train soon arrived at Rotterdam station. Rotterdam is very different from Amsterdam, and you see the differences as soon as you reach it by train. Rotterdam is just like any other modern city, with tall glass buildings and apartment blocks. It has none of the beauty of Amsterdam with its lovely old buildings and canals.

I met Tom Carson at the club offices. He was a slim grey-haired man of about fifty and he looked so much like Max that I suddenly felt sad. Tom had the body of a sportsman. He had played for Ajax when he was younger, and he still looked like he could kick a ball around a field.

'It's really good of you to see me,' I said. 'I'm so sorry about Max.'

'Yes, it's awful,' said Tom Carson. 'Hard to believe really. Just senseless.' Max's brother shook his head. He looked tired.

'Max was a wonderful man,' I said.

We talked about Max a little and our time together in Manchester. Then Tom Carson asked, 'What can I do for you, Miss Jensen?'

'Well, I want to write something about a Dutch football club, comparing it to an English club,' I explained. 'You know, training – that sort of thing. Rotterdam City seems like a good choice. But perhaps it's not a good time ... '

I didn't tell Carson that Max had wanted me to come and write a story about the club.

'No, it's fine,' he said. 'Life goes on. We have to think about the future of the club. The boys are going to start training in a few minutes.'

Although he was sad at his brother's death, Tom Carson did not want to miss the opportunity of some good publicity for his club. He was a good businessman, I thought.

We walked out to the training ground and sat at the side. The 'boys' started coming out from a dressing room under the offices.

'They're getting ready for a European Cup game right now. They play Barcelona here at home tomorrow evening,' he explained.

I wondered how they would play against Barcelona after their terrible match against Leiden. Barcelona were one of the best teams in Europe. If they couldn't win against Leiden, what hope did they have against 'Barca'?

'I think they'll be OK,' said Carson, as if reading my thoughts. But I had the feeling that he didn't really believe it.

The players were doing their warm-up exercises out on the field. The sun was shining and there was a light wind, as usual in Holland. We talked about the training and I watched the team a bit more, hoping that Carson wouldn't realise how little I knew about football.

'The interesting thing,' said Carson, 'is the school and the team – you know, having both. It makes us different.'

'Yes, it sounds interesting,' I said. 'I'd really like to visit the school if possible.'

Carson smiled. 'Well, that couldn't be easier, Miss Jensen. It's just down the road. I'll take you myself,' he said. Before leaving, I looked once more at the team on the field. The players were practising crossing the ball to the strikers, who then shot at goal. The strikers were strong and mostly managed to get the ball into the goal.

'They look good,' I said to Tom Carson. 'I guess you're hoping for a few goals tomorrow night.'

Carson gave a worried smile.

Tom Carson showed me round the Carson Football School. The boys lived at the school. They slept there, ate there, studied there and played football there. It was modern and clean, with very good teaching plus football training that Tom said was 'first class'. The boys were everywhere, studying and playing football. They were quite young, between eight and fifteen I guessed, though there were two or three older ones.

'A lot of them come from very poor families, Miss Jensen,' said Tom, as we watched a group of ten boys doing some practice. They were kicking the ball round some boxes that had been placed in a line, then getting to the end and shooting at the goal. They looked good, I thought. Good sportspeople are all the same in some ways. It doesn't matter whether they do karate, play tennis or play football. They have good balance and keep their heads very still.

'Some of the boys are Dutch, but some come from South America and Africa. We find young boys who are really good and bring them back here,' he continued.

'And that was what Max did?' I asked.

'Yes,' he said. 'Max looked for kids like these, and also good players in other teams.'

I took some notes for my 'story' and looked around a little more. The boys certainly looked happy and well cared for.

'And most of them become professional footballers?' I asked.

'Most of them,' he said. 'If they're good enough.'

Tom Carson and I left the school. I shook his hand, said goodbye and went back to Rotterdam station. On the train back to Amsterdam it was hard not to think about the manager's sad smile. Carson was unhappy, I thought, and not only because he'd just lost his brother.

Chapter 8 *Life gets interesting*

Back in Amsterdam, I went to the main public library – I had some detective work to do. It was time to find out exactly who had money in Rotterdam City Football Club. Max had told me that he had about twenty-five per cent of the shares in the club, but was the club owned just by the Carson brothers?

The library assistant showed me to a computer where I could get onto the Internet and I began work. I searched for information about Rotterdam City Football Club over the past five or six years. Two hours later, I was beginning to build up a picture of what had happened to the club.

It was interesting reading. Tom Carson's shares in the club had gone down from seventy-five per cent to just thirty per cent over the past two years. But Tom's shares hadn't gone to Max. Max's shares remained at twenty-five per cent during the whole time he was at the club. Most of the shares had gone to someone called Martijn Christiaans. I looked back over the past few years. Christiaans had started buying shares two years ago and had started with just ten per cent, but he now owned forty-five per cent of Rotterdam City Football Club.

Who was Martijn Christiaans, I wondered, and why was Tom Carson allowing him to buy up his club?

I wondered what had happened to Max's shares now. No doubt they had passed straight to Tom Carson. With Max dead, his brother now had fifty-five per cent of the club – a very strong position to be in.

I left the public library. It was time for a bit more detective work.

I started with the telephone book back in my hotel room. I was lucky. I found just one Martijn Christiaans in the book, with an address on Herengracht. I went to take a look.

Herengracht was just a five-minute walk away from the hotel. As I walked I thought of the story that I would tell Christiaans if he was at home. I was writing a story on old buildings in Amsterdam and I wanted to talk to him about his house. I knew that Herengracht was full of wonderful old houses. I arrived at number 141 and looked up at the top of the house as if I was suddenly interested in old buildings. It was beautiful. Probably 17th century, and in very good condition. Christiaans was obviously extremely rich.

I took a deep breath and went up the steps to the door. It was made of beautiful black wood and there was a silver bell above the name. I rang the bell, waited, then rang again. There was no-one at home.

Just as I was turning to go, a young woman of about twenty-five arrived at the next house, carrying shopping bags. She said something to me in Dutch, so I said, 'Sorry, I don't understand.'

'Oh, sorry,' said the woman, smiling at me. 'I said if you're looking for Mr Christiaans, I saw him going out early this morning.'

'Do you know what kind of work he does?' I asked.

'Mmm, I'm not really sure. I don't know him very well.'

And with that she opened the door of her house and went inside.

It seemed I'd missed Christiaans, so I went back to the hotel. There I had better luck. There was a letter waiting for me at reception. It had been posted yesterday in the city and had arrived in the second post. The name and address on the envelope had been typed. It just said 'Miss Jensen', then the name and address of the hotel. I opened the envelope. Inside there was a short note, written by hand in capital letters:

DEAR MISS JENSEN

YOU SHOULD LOOK INTO THE MONEY THAT WAS BET ON

LEIDEN TO WIN THE MATCH AGAINST ROTTERDAM

A FREIND

I didn't know who had written the letter, but it was someone who couldn't spell 'friend'.

'Good news?' asked the young woman at reception.

'Maybe . . . ' I said.

Who had bet on Leiden to win the match? Where could I find out? I rang Elly.

'Now, let's see,' said Elly. 'Most of the betting on sport is done through a betting office called Kanters. Try a guy called Ronnie in the office here in Amsterdam and give him my name. He owes me something. He should be able to help you.' Then she added, 'And be careful, Kate.'

A few minutes after talking to Elly, I rang Jos van Essen.

'Miss Jensen, what a surprise!' he said.

'Mr van Essen,' I said, 'I was wondering . . . I've heard

that Rotterdam are playing Barcelona tomorrow and, well, I'd like to see the match.' I knew that as an ex-player he would have tickets.

'Well ... yes, of course. Why not come with me?' he asked.

'That would be great!' I said.

'Good. I'll pick you up at your hotel around 5.30. The match starts at 7.30. Goodnight,' said the beautiful striker.

I put the phone down. Life, I thought, was beginning to look interesting.

* * *

That evening life suddenly got even more interesting. At about 10.30 I decided to go out for a walk. I needed some air and I needed to think. It was dark by now and there were very few people walking around near the hotel. I walked slowly down Keizersgracht, staring at the pavement, thinking about everything that had happened during the day. I walked down by the canal.

Suddenly a car stopped in the street next to me. A dark shape jumped out, came up behind me and pulled my arm behind my back. It hurt like hell. 'Get in the car and don't make a noise, or I'll break your arm,' the guy said. I didn't recognise the voice.

I raised my foot and kicked the guy hard in his right leg. At the same time I pulled back my free arm and put my elbow into his chest. My attacker wasn't expecting this and it worked well, taking his breath away.

The guy let go and I turned round quickly. I looked up and saw a tall dark-haired man with clear blue eyes.

'Come here,' he said. He pulled me, trying to get me into the car.

'Hey, say please,' I said, fighting back. He was smiling, almost making fun of me. That made me really mad. He was quite strong, and much bigger than me, but my years of karate training had made me fast. I also knew how to surprise him.

He managed to pull me nearer to the car. I stepped back on my left foot, pulled up my right leg quickly and gave him a karate kick in the stomach, with my right foot. I put all my weight behind the kick and it surprised him. He was tall, but if you hit the stomach, size doesn't matter. He started to fall over like a tree and, as he fell, I hit him on the side of his head with my elbow. The elbow is the hardest bone in the body and in no time he was on his knees, holding his head between his hands. He realised then that it was not going to be as easy as he had thought. He hadn't expected me to put up such a fight. He quickly climbed back into his car looking around nervously. He was probably afraid that the noise would bring people out to see what was happening.

He was going to get away. I looked around to see if there was anyone who could get help, but the street was empty. I wanted to stop him, but there was no way I could stop him on my own. The next moment there was a screeching noise as my attacker started his car, put his foot down hard, and raced off down the road.

Chapter 9 *The Amsterdam Connection*

I ran up the stairs to my room and locked the door behind me, breathing heavily. I guessed that this guy had been outside the hotel, watching me, waiting for his chance. I took a whisky from the mini-bar in my room and drank it quickly. I went to bed, but I slept badly.

The next day I planned to go to see Ronnie, Elly's 'friend' at Kanters. But before I could leave my hotel room, I got another surprise. Elly came to the hotel on her way to work. The Amsterdam police had got the results of Max's postmortem. A friend of hers in de Vries's team had told her about it.

'They're saying he definitely died of the knife wounds,' she said. 'He lost a lot of blood. And it's ninety-five per cent certain that he died there, in de Pijp.'

'And they still think it's this guy Schaap?' I asked.

'Yes,' she said. 'Although they haven't found the knife.'

I told Elly what Bert had told me. Elly just looked at me. She didn't have to say anything. We both knew that it was more than possible that Bert was telling lies just to get money.

'What about the time of death?' I asked her.

'They're not completely sure, but it was somewhere between midnight and 3.30 in the morning,' said Elly.

I didn't tell Elly anything about what had happened the night before. She left to go to work and I left to go to Kanters. Outside the hotel I looked around me and then stopped a taxi. From now on I had to be careful.

At the Kanters office I asked to see Ronnie. A young woman led me into a back office where Ronnie sat working at a computer. He just carried on staring at the computer when I went in, hardly looking at me. The office was dark, with just a small window at the back. Ronnie was a thin little man of about forty, with almost no hair. His skin was white and he looked unhealthy. I guessed he spent most of his time working in this dark room. I explained what I wanted.

'I can't give you that type of information,' he said, without looking up.

I said Elly's name. It worked. He turned round, looked me up and down, then closed the door so that no-one from the front office could hear us. I don't know what he owed Elly, but it was obviously something big.

'Come back in an hour,' he said in a low voice.

I went out, bought a newspaper and went into a café. I looked at the sports pages. There was a report about tonight's match and I read what I could. I looked out of the window, drank my coffee and thought.

If Max had been knifed somewhere else, as Bert said, what about the blood? The blood would be in the car, everywhere. That meant a bloody car left somewhere, or a big clean-up.

I went back to see Ronnie, who by now had the information on his computer screen. I had told him that I was looking for a big bet, a large amount of money on Leiden to win the match against Rotterdam.

'Everybody expected Rotterdam to win,' said Ronnie. 'They were the favourites. Leiden were six to one. That means that if you bet a guilder, you got six guilders,' he explained.

I smiled. 'Oh really?' I said. Sometimes it was best to let people believe that you understood nothing.

'Here we are,' he said suddenly. 'Here's something that might interest you. Some big bets on Leiden. There are three bets of half a million guilders.' That was almost £200,000.

I went round to look at the computer screen. The bets had been placed by a betting syndicate, or group, and there were no names of people. The bets had been placed in Amsterdam, Leiden and Rotterdam. The name of the syndicate was the Amsterdam Connection.

The name meant nothing to me.

'Wow!' I said. 'One and a half million guilders ... that's over half a million pounds in total ... That's a really big bet. Is that usual?'

'Well,' said Ronnie, 'it's not that common, but it does happen. And it's allowed. We never ask questions – it's not our job.'

The Amsterdam Connection were probably very happy that no-one asked questions. At six to one, they had made about £3,000,000! Not bad for a night's work.

I asked Ronnie for a list of all the bets placed by the Amsterdam Connection in the past year. He said it would take him a day. I said I'd be back next morning, early.

'Oh, and tonight's match too. I want to find out if there are any large bets on Barcelona,' I said as I left.

I went back to the hotel and lay on my bed to think. I turned on the TV. There was a football match on. I didn't know who the teams were, but I watched for a while. A blond-haired striker had the ball. He went past three men and shot at goal. The goalkeeper went to his right to save the ball but missed. The blond guy had scored a fantastic goal and jumped up and down.

The goalkeeper . . . I wondered. I turned off the TV and smiled to myself.

Chapter 10 *A policeman*

'And what makes you think,' asked de Vries, 'that this betting syndicate, the Amsterdam Connection, has got anything to do with Mr Christiaans?'

I was talking to Inspector Joop de Vries, head of the Amsterdam Police Murder Squad, at police headquarters on Elandsgracht. It was time, I had decided, to see if we could work together. But he was a tall unsmiling man and he wasn't easy to talk to – I could see why Elly didn't like him.

'It's a guess,' I said, 'but I think it's worth looking into.'

De Vries stared at me. He wasn't a man who liked to guess. I could see that I wasn't getting anywhere. And it wasn't very pleasant sitting in his office. It was filled with cigarette smoke and his desk was a mess.

'And then there's this guy that I met in de Pijp . . . ' I said.

'This guy?' de Vries asked, putting another cigarette in his mouth.

'Yes, I can't tell you his name, but – '

'Miss Jensen,' said de Vries, trying to be patient, 'how can I accept the word of someone whose name I do not know?

There was silence for a moment. I wanted to leave right then, but decided to try a little longer.

'But he says that Max Carson was already dead when he

arrived in de Pijp,' I said, 'and the guy that you've got, this Schaap guy – he just stole his wallet.'

De Vries said nothing.

'And then I was attacked, on the street outside my hotel,' I said. 'Somebody was trying to frighten me.'

I was sure that whoever had attacked me was trying to stop me from finding the truth.

'I'm very sorry about that Miss Jensen,' said de Vries. 'Amsterdam is quite a safe city, but these things do happen.'

I wondered how I was going to make this man understand.

'And the evidence?' he continued, blowing cigarette smoke over his desk into my face. 'Where's your evidence? The only thing you have is the story of a man who is almost certainly a criminal himself.'

'I don't have any evidence yet. That's my problem,' I said calmly. 'Anyway, I'm not a policewoman, Inspector, I'm a news reporter. You're the ones who are supposed to find the evidence,' I reminded him.

That was a mistake. De Vries was not the kind of guy who liked to be told how to do his job. 'Now look, Miss Jensen,' he said, suddenly sitting up straight. 'I suggest you keep to your job and I'll keep to mine. We work with evidence around here. As you say, you are not a policewoman. Perhaps it's best to keep out of it. You people just make our job more difficult,' he added.

The police were the same in Holland as they were in England, I thought. Always complaining about reporters.

'Look, Inspector,' I said, trying to stay calm, 'I've come here to give you some information. There's nothing in it for me. I just thought you might look into it.'

I stood up to leave. I got the feeling that I was talking to myself and wasting a lot of time. I had to get hold of some evidence. I left de Vries in his smoky office sitting at his messy desk. I had a football match to see.

Chapter 11 *A football match*

'Who's the Rotterdam goalkeeper?' I asked Jos van Essen as we drove to Rotterdam in his white Porsche.

'Raúl Sanchez,' he said. 'Why?'

'Tell me about him,' I said.

'A great goalkeeper, a nice guy,' said Jos.

'No, I mean . . . his family and things,' I said.

'Oh, well. He comes from Colombia. His family were very poor. I think when the Carson School found him, he was a boy of eight or nine. He was working on the street in Bogotá,' said Jos, as he turned onto the motorway to Rotterdam.

'And the Carson School arranged for his whole family to come to Holland, right?' I asked.

'No, not exactly. They still live over there, but Raúl has enough money for them to live comfortably now.'

That was a big responsibility for a young man, I thought. Raúl Sanchez had to make sure that his family were all right.

Since watching the match on television I had been thinking a lot about goalkeepers. Strikers were important when it came to winning and losing matches, but goalkeepers were important too. If you wanted a team to lose a match, the goalkeeper was the man for the job.

Jos and I chatted about this and that as we drove to Rotterdam. Jos told me about his plans for the future. Perhaps he would go to England to manage a football team and start a new life there. He'd had offers from some big clubs.

At about 6.50 we arrived at Rotterdam Football Club. We left the car in the car park and went towards the stadium.

'We must hurry,' said Jos, 'or we'll miss the start of the match.'

We went into the crowded stadium and found our seats. As an ex-player, Jos had tickets for the best seats. I looked around. There were probably fifty thousand people. There was a lot of noise with the fans of both teams singing and shouting.

Less than a minute after we'd sat down, the referee blew his whistle and the match started. Rotterdam played well in the first half of the match and got the first goal. Their star striker, Ritter, scored with his favourite left foot, the ball flying into the corner of the goal. The Barcelona goalkeeper went towards the ball, but couldn't reach it. At half time the score was 1–0 to Rotterdam. The Rotterdam fans screamed and shouted.

In the second half, it was Barcelona who played better, though for a while nobody shot at goal. Then, after about seventy-five minutes' play, their great striker, Martínez, finally started a run. He went round one, two, three men. The Barcelona fans screamed, 'Martínez! Martínez!' Martínez was in front of the goal. He shot into the top right-hand corner. The Rotterdam goalkeeper, Sanchez, jumped towards the ball but it went through his fingers and into the goal. It was 1–1! The Barcelona fans went crazy.

Then, about ten minutes later, Martínez scored again. Again, Sanchez touched the ball, but it went through his fingers. Sanchez wasn't playing well at all. The Barcelona fans went even more crazy! Then the referee blew the final whistle. Barcelona had won 2–1!

We hurried out of the stadium as quickly as we could, trying to avoid the crowds. 'Thank you,' I said to Jos as he started the car to go back to Amsterdam. 'It was great!' Even though Rotterdam had lost, it had been exciting. I hadn't been to a football match since Max had taken me to see Manchester United years before.

Jos didn't look too happy. 'Barcelona are a great team, but Rotterdam should have won. Well, let's hope they do better against Ajax.'

'When are they playing Ajax?' I asked. Ajax were the team from Amsterdam.

'Saturday,' Jos answered. 'Only three days away. And it's a big one. It's important Rotterdam win.'

We drove back to Amsterdam, talking about the match.

Finally we reached the Continental. As the car stopped outside the hotel, Jos said, 'Oh, I've got something for you, Kate.'

He picked up a large brown envelope lying on the back seat. In the envelope was a copy of the photograph I had seen at Jos's apartment in Oude Schans – the photo of the Rotterdam team.

'I saw you liked it,' he said, smiling. 'So here's one for you.' He handed it to me.

'Oh, thank you,' I said. 'That's really kind of you, Jos. Could you sign your name on the back for me, perhaps with a little message?'

'Of course.' Jos pulled a pen out of his pocket and

turned the photograph over. 'What would you like me to write?'

'Why not "To my friend, Kate"?' I suggested.

'My dear friend,' said Jos, smiling.

He wrote the message, put the photograph back in the envelope and gave it to me. 'Goodnight, Kate,' he said.

I got out of the car and watched him drive away. Then I took the photograph out of the envelope and looked down at it. It read: 'To my dear freind Kate, with love from Jos.'

My mind was racing. So Jos was my 'freind'. He knew, or thought he knew, something about what was going on. I just hoped his information was better than his spelling.

I walked into the hotel lost in thought. I needed to speak to Jos. I decided I would go and see him the next day.

But the next day never came for Jos van Essen. That night he was found dead outside his apartment on Oude Schans.

Chapter 12 *A goalkeeper*

'Let's start with the Amsterdam Connection,' I said to Raúl Sanchez, the goalkeeper at Rotterdam City Football Club.

'What?' he asked.

Sanchez was a handsome man with dark brown skin and lots of curly black hair. His brown eyes looked surprised, but I had a feeling that he knew exactly what I was talking about. I explained, though, just to make really sure.

'The Amsterdam Connection,' I explained, 'is the name of a syndicate, a group of people who are putting big money on football teams that play against Rotterdam City. They're making millions.'

I was talking to Sanchez at his house just outside Amsterdam. It was Friday. Jos van Essen had been found, stabbed to death outside his apartment the day before. His wallet had gone. Again, the killing looked just like a mugging. I was angry and I wanted answers.

'I don't know what you're talking about, Miss Jensen,' said Sanchez. 'I think you'd better leave.' He got up.

'Sit down,' I said. 'I'm not going anywhere until I find out what's going on.'

The goalkeeper sat down.

'Listen Raúl, and listen well,' I continued seriously. 'Two of my friends are dead and I'm angry. Very angry. I know that someone is betting large amounts of money on Rotterdam losing matches.'

'And so?' he asked.

'I know that you are a great goalkeeper who played like a five-year-old last night. I also know,' I added, just so that he understood clearly, 'that if I tell the police what I know and you don't help them, that you will go to prison for a very long time. And I will tell the police. You'll lose your career as a footballer and your family will be poor again. You choose.'

I looked at him. He sat staring down at his feet. He didn't say anything for a long time, but finally I saw that my words were beginning to work. Or perhaps it was Jos van Essen's death that was helping the Rotterdam goalkeeper to see that he was playing a dangerous game.

'Well, yes ... ' said Sanchez, taking a deep breath. 'I've been offered a lot of money to, you know, lose matches.'

Sanchez looked unhappy.

'You were asked to lose matches?' I repeated.

I knew it happened sometimes in football and in other sports. Back in England, there had been a big case with a London club about two years before. Criminals had offered famous players money to lose matches: to miss goals if they were strikers or miss the ball if they were goalkeepers. Then the criminals put a lot of money on the other team to win. They had made millions of pounds that way before they were caught. And of course the players could get sent to prison, too.

'Yes,' said Sanchez quietly, 'but ... '

'But you want to stop, right?' I asked.

The goalkeeper nodded.

'And you were asked to lose matches by Tom Carson?' I asked.

'No, no, not Mr Carson,' he said.

'Well, who was it?' I asked.

'Christiaans,' he said. 'Martijn Christiaans.' I looked across at Sanchez. His face had gone almost white – he was a frightened man.

So that's what Christiaans was doing: taking over the club and making millions for himself, possibly with the help of some friends. But why was Tom Carson letting him do it? Perhaps Tom Carson, too, was frightened of Christiaans. But why?

'Does Tom know what Christiaans is doing?' I asked.

'Yes, of course ... Well, he must know,' said Sanchez. 'But he can't do anything to stop him, I'm not sure why, but he just can't.'

'So why didn't you go to the police at the start?' I said.

'I was too frightened,' said Sanchez.

'Frightened?' I asked.

'Of course,' he said, looking worried. 'I could lose everything. I have four brothers and sisters who would have to leave school and go back on the street. And my mother would be very poor again.'

Poor Sanchez. He was in an impossible situation.

'And Christiaans is a dangerous guy,' he added, his brown eyes growing larger. 'I mean very dangerous. You saw what happened to Max and Jos van Essen.'

It was obvious why everyone was frightened.

'I've known for a long time that I have to stop this,' said the Rotterdam goalkeeper. 'I just don't know how.'

'And the match against Ajax tomorrow,' I said. 'Have you been asked to lose that one as well?'

'Yes,' he said quietly. Again fear came into his eyes.

'Don't worry,' I said to Sanchez. 'I think we can do

something. But we have to act quickly and we need some evidence, something to show the police.'

Once again, my only hope was Elly. I rang her.

'Listen, Elly,' I said, 'I need your help again.'

'Well, I'm busy right now, Kate,' she said. 'I can be there in an hour.'

I gave her the address of Sanchez's house and put the phone down.

An hour later Elly was sitting looking at Sanchez and me, listening carefully. I told her the whole story. I could see from her face that she believed me.

'So, Elly,' I asked, 'do you think you can get us a tape recorder and a microphone? You know, the kind you can put in a pocket or something.'

I knew that the police used tiny microphones and tape recorders that you could hide in bags, or pockets, or even attach to a person's clothes. Elly said she thought she could get one.

'Elly,' I said, 'there's another thing.'

'Yes?' she asked.

'Max Carson had a bad heart. Jos told me that he took pills. I need to know if the police found the pills in his room or on his body. I need to know how many pills were in the bottle, the name of the chemist where he got them and the date,' I said.

'Is that all?' she asked.

'Yeah, and if you could get the information quickly . . . ' I said, giving her my sweetest smile.

Chapter 13 *A plan*

Elly returned an hour later with the tape recorder and microphone.

'Now here's what I want you to do,' I said to Raúl. 'We're going to attach this microphone and tape recorder to the inside of your jacket. Just remember to stay close to Christiaans while he's speaking.'

Then Raúl rang Christiaans and arranged to see him at his house. 'I just want to talk about something,' said Raúl cheerfully.

When he got to Christiaans' house, Raúl was going to tell him that he wanted more money for playing badly. We all hoped that Christiaans would talk, say something about what he was doing while Raúl taped him. It was very dangerous for Raúl, but if it worked it would give us the evidence we needed.

'I'll go with Raúl,' said Elly. 'I'll wait nearby.'

After the interview with Christiaans, Elly could also make sure that Raúl didn't get hurt. She had brought some jeans and a blouse and she now changed from her policewoman's uniform.

'Oh,' I added, 'and what about the pills? Did you find out anything?'

'Yes, the police did find some pills in Max's room,' she said. 'They were called Lanoxin. They were bought from a chemist in The Hague two weeks ago. The full bottle was sixty pills and you have to take just one a day. There were about thirty left when they found them.'

Lanoxin ... Lanoxin ... I knew that name from somewhere, but right now I couldn't remember where.

Elly and Raúl left. It was time for me to go and see Ronnie at Kanters.

I took a taxi to the Kanters office. When I got there, Ronnie was sitting at his computer, exactly as I had seen him yesterday. It was like he never went home. He had a computer print-out of the information I needed.

I looked at the print-out. It was very interesting reading. There were, as I had thought, regular bets against Rotterdam over the past year made by the Amsterdam Connection. There was also a large bet on Barcelona to win Wednesday's match. The Amsterdam Connection had done it again. However, a far larger amount of money was on the Rotterdam–Ajax match taking place the next day.

I put the computer print-out in an envelope and posted it to my hotel, with my name on it. That way, whatever happened, it would arrive at the hotel tomorrow.

I went back to the hotel to wait for Elly and Raúl to come back. I ordered some tea from room service and waited. I drank my tea. An hour went by. Then two hours. As time went on I became more and more worried. Where were they? We had arranged to meet back at the hotel as soon as they had the tape with the evidence on it. I tried to read, then watch TV, but I couldn't. My mind filled up with terrible ideas of what had happened to them.

I lay on my bed and tried to relax. The name of Max's pills came into my head again. Lanoxin. Yes! That was it! Lanoxin contains digoxin, a powerful heart drug which can kill you if you take too much of it. I had first heard about Lanoxin during a story in London. A doctor had killed his wife using it. It's perfect for killing someone because digoxin can't be found in the body after about twelve hours. Perhaps someone had made Max take a lot of Lanoxin pills and killed him that way! Perhaps Bert was right after all. Perhaps Max had been dead before someone knifed him in de Pijp.

Then, finally, at about seven o'clock, there was a knock at the door. Thank God, I thought. I jumped up and opened it, expecting to see Elly and Raúl. Suddenly I was pushed back into the room. A tall man in a black suit moved quickly through the door and put his hand over my mouth. It was the same man who had attacked me outside the hotel three days ago. The same dark hair and clear blue eyes.

'Christiaans?' I asked.

'Keep quiet!' he said into my ear. 'Or I'll kill you.'

I took that as a 'yes'.

Chapter 14 *Prisoner*

Christiaans pushed me to the other side of the room. I saw that he was holding a gun. 'Where is it?' he said.

'Where's what?' I asked, trying to look calm.

'The print-out!' he said. 'I've just visited your friend Ronnie and I don't think he'll be helping you any more. Now where is it?'

'Where are Elly and Raúl? What have you done to them?' I shouted. I was angry.

He smiled an ugly smile. 'They're fine,' he said. 'But they are very stupid. Raúl should know better than to go against me, and your policewoman friend should stay away from things she knows nothing about.'

'Where are they?' I said again. I wanted to hit him but the gun was pointing right at me.

'They're quite safe. We need Raúl to be fit if he's going to play his best, or should I say worst, for us tomorrow.'

'He'll never do it,' I said.

'Oh, I think he will,' said Christiaans, smiling again. 'If he wants you and Elly to live.'

'It'll never work,' I said. 'Elly will be missed at police headquarters.'

'It's Saturday tomorrow,' he said. 'Who'll miss her? By the time anyone misses her or you, the match will be over, I'll be a multimillionaire and I'll be far away from here. Now,' he continued, looking serious again, 'it's time you joined your friends. I need you safely out of the way until the match is over. Come on, we're going for a little walk outside. And remember, this gun is pointing at you. If you make any noise at all, it will be a pleasure to shoot you.'

Before we left the room, he hid the gun under his coat and held it against my back. Then he pushed me out of the door, down the stairs and through the back door of the hotel. He was tall and strong. With him standing just behind me and his gun in my back, it would be stupid to try anything. Outside the hotel he pushed me into the back of a small van with dark windows. Then there was nothing.

* * *

The first thing I noticed was the pain; a terrible pain starting at the back of my head and finishing over my eyes.

At first it seemed as if I was in complete darkness. Then my eyes got used to it and above me I could see a little light coming from a window. It was hard to think with the pain in my head, but I guessed that I was lying on the floor of a room under a house, a cellar perhaps. The floor was made of stone and it was hard, dirty and cold.

I checked my body. This was difficult because I was handcuffed – my hands held together in front of me. The hard metal of the handcuffs cut into my hands. Other than the terrible headache, I seemed to be OK. Then my eyes got more used to the dark and I looked around the room. There, in the corner, was Elly, wearing handcuffs and with something over her mouth so that she couldn't speak. Her eyes were shut, but I saw that she was breathing; she wasn't dead but I guessed she was unconscious. She had blood running from her head. I wondered where Raúl was.

I had to think and act quickly. What would happen once the match was over and Christiaans had his money? I couldn't see someone like Christiaans letting us go. I was quite sure he'd kill us anyway. Maybe he'd make our murders look like senseless stabbings, leaving our bodies in the street at night. That was what he had done with Max and Jos. From what he had said, he obviously had a flight booked to some country far away once the match was over. Perhaps he'd just leave us in this cellar to die.

I went to Elly and spoke to her. At first she didn't move but then, slowly, her eyes opened a little. She looked at me as if she hardly knew me.

'Listen, Elly,' I whispered. 'It's me, Kate. I'm going to try to get out of here, but I'll come back soon, OK? I'll come back with help.'

Her eyes closed again.

I heard voices somewhere. I knew that I didn't have much time. I had to get out of here, and find a way of getting Elly out, too. It seemed impossible.

I looked up again towards the window. Yes, I thought, we were in a cellar and that window probably faced the street. There would also probably be steps which led up to the street. These cellars were very common in Amsterdam. The window was about two metres above me and very small. Luckily it was open a little and there was a stone shelf just beneath it. It wasn't very wide, but it was just wide enough perhaps. If only I could reach that shelf! But how? And even if I could manage to reach it, how was I going to get through the window? I was quite slim, but the window looked very small.

I walked slowly to the wall where the window was and

felt it with the back of my hand. I moved my hands slowly up the wall, trying to find somewhere I could place a foot. There was nothing.

I moved backwards, away from the window, towards a corner of the room. As I moved in the darkness I almost fell over something behind me. It was a chair! It was old and it didn't seem very strong, but it was a chair. I started to pull it carefully towards the little window. It was my only hope.

It was hard to move the chair without making any noise. Any movement on the floor made a lot of noise and the metal handcuffs stopped me from lifting the chair. I tried to breathe slowly. It took a long time but finally the chair was in position under the window. It was time to try it out, to see if it would take my weight. If it wasn't strong enough and I fell, the people upstairs would certainly hear the noise and come running to the cellar. It would be the end.

First I sat on it. It was fine. Then I stepped up onto the chair, slowly and carefully. To my surprise it didn't break. I reached up to the window and managed to touch it. It was dark outside, and I guessed it must be very late. I must have been unconscious for a long time.

Just then I heard a low noise behind me. I turned. It was Elly trying to speak.

'Shh! Elly,' I whispered. 'I'll be back soon, I promise.' As I said it, I wondered whether it was true, whether I could really promise that.

I turned back towards the window. I felt the night air coming through it and heard the sound of traffic somewhere. Rain, too. It had started raining. Perhaps I could get through the window, I thought. I would have to pull myself up as hard as I could. If I fell back onto the chair there would be a lot of noise and we would be finished.

I reached up and pulled as hard as I could. I slowly managed to lift myself up onto the shelf just below the window. My arms were strong after all the years of karate training. I felt the fresh air on my face. I breathed it in, trying to give myself new strength. I looked back at Elly. If I could escape, perhaps I could get help.

I pushed through the window, handcuffed hands first, then head. I could see the ground just a metre below me. But would I get through that tiny window?

I pushed my knees against the shelf, breathing heavily. I gave one final strong push and I was out! I pushed my hands down to the ground and fell on my shoulder. I had been right about the steps. I was lying at the bottom of about ten stone steps. I stood up quickly and ran up the steps and out onto the street. I looked up at the house. I had seen it before – it was Christiaans' house on Herengracht. I ran as fast as I could down the street. It was raining very hard now. I just kept on running.

I ran all the way to the central police station on Elandsgracht. The young policeman at the desk looked at me very strangely as I ran through the door. I was wet from head to foot and wearing handcuffs. I quickly told the policeman what was happening as he took the handcuffs off. 'We have to get back to Herengracht quickly,' I said. 'Very quickly! Christiaans is dangerous!'

The policeman called three other policemen. I got into a car with two of them and two others followed in another car. As we drove to Herengracht, I told the policemen more of the story. I told them I didn't know where Raúl was and that I was worried about him. Five minutes later, we parked just round the corner from Christiaans' house.

Two of the policemen went round to the front of the house; the other two ran off round the back. The idea was that as the two policemen rang the bell at the front of the house, the two at the back would kick the door down and rescue Elly.

I sat in the car, shaking with the cold. The policeman had given me a blanket and I pulled it around me, trying to get warm. I could see the two policemen at the back of the house. There was a loud noise as they broke the door down. Then there was silence. Each minute seemed like an hour. Suddenly I heard a gunshot! Who had been shot? 'Please, God, don't let it be Elly,' I said to myself. I listened for more shots, but I heard nothing.

Finally, after about fifteen minutes, two of the policemen came out of the house with Christiaans handcuffed. There was blood coming from Christiaans' leg. I sat forward, hoping that I would soon see Elly. Then, a few moments later, the other two policemen came out with Elly. Behind her was Raúl! So he had been in the house all the time! He looked OK. Elly looked pretty bad, but she was alive.

One of the policemen helped Elly into the car next to me and Raúl got in on the other side.

'Thank God you're safe,' I said and took hold of Elly's hand.

She gave me a weak smile.

'So what happened?' I asked them.

'Well, everything went as planned,' said Raúl.

'Christiaans talked to me and I left his house with the tape.'

'Yes,' said Elly, 'and then Raúl came outside and round the corner to meet me. But Christiaans followed him. He had a gun and made us go back to his house. I think Christiaans was very clever. He probably realised that something was going on as soon as Raúl said he wanted to visit him.'

'When we got back into the house, he knocked Elly out and locked me in another room,' said Raúl. 'He needed me to play in the match. And he needed Elly – he told me that he'd kill her if I didn't play and lose the match against Ajax.'

It was lucky that Raúl was an important part of Christiaans' plan. If he hadn't been, both he and Elly would probably have been killed there and then.

Chapter 15 *Stories*

It was 3.00 in the morning and I was sitting in de Vries's smoky office with Elly. She had seen a doctor at the police station and was feeling a little better. De Vries was angry that she had put herself in so much danger, but mainly he was just happy that she was OK.

Raúl had told his whole story to de Vries and was allowed to go home. He would have to give evidence later, but he probably wouldn't be sent to prison.

My head was hurting, but at last I was giving de Vries the evidence he wanted, the evidence that would send Christiaans to prison for a very long time.

'Max Carson wouldn't play Christiaans' game,' I said. 'Max had found out what was going on. He tried to get Christiaans to stop, but he couldn't. My guess is that Christiaans was the person Max was going to visit that Thursday evening. Probably to tell him to stop or to warn him that he would tell the police. Christiaans couldn't allow that so he killed him.'

'So he stabbed Max in his house?' de Vries asked.

'No,' I answered. 'The guy I met in de Pijp was right; Max was dead before he was knifed. Somehow Christiaans made Max take far too much Lanoxin, Max's heart pills. Perhaps he put the pills into a drink.'

I told him about digoxin; about how you couldn't find it in the body after twelve hours. 'There were a lot of pills missing from Max's bottle,' I said.

'But why then stab him?' de Vries asked.

'Well, Christiaans had a body to get rid of somehow,' I explained. 'He didn't want to leave it in the street just like it was because the police would wonder how Max had died. You would probably have done a postmortem immediately and found the drug still in Max's body. Christiaans decided it would be much safer to make you think Max had been stabbed to death by a street criminal.'

'And it almost worked,' said Elly. 'By the time the postmortem was done, the drug couldn't be found.'

De Vries looked at me. 'And van Essen?' he asked.

'Well, unfortunately he knew too much,' I said. 'He'd refused to take money from Christiaans and had tried to keep out of it. He even left the football club that he loved. I think he was very sad to see what was happening to football. He had his dreams . . .

'But it was hard to just forget about it,' I continued. 'He liked Max and he knew that he was in a difficult situation. And then Max was killed and Jos was sure Christiaans had murdered him . . . And then I came.' I stopped. I wondered whether Jos van Essen would still be alive if I hadn't arrived in Amsterdam, if I hadn't made him part of it again. I suddenly felt very sad.

'And,' I added, 'you can see the evidence about the Amsterdam Connection when it arrives in the post tomorrow – I mean today!'

Christiaans had probably destroyed the evidence on the computer at Kanters, but at least there was a paper copy. Then I remembered Ronnie. What had happened to him?

'He's OK,' said de Vries. 'Christiaans hurt him a little and frightened him a lot, but he didn't kill him.'

'And what about the rest of the Amsterdam Connection?' I asked. I guessed that Christiaans had about three or four 'friends' who were part of the syndicate.

De Vries smiled. 'We're looking for them now, Miss Jensen,' he said.

'There's just one thing that I don't really understand,' Elly said. 'Why did Tom Carson allow Christiaans to buy up his club?'

'Yes,' I said. 'I'd like to know that, too.'

'Well, why don't we ask him?' said de Vries. 'He's in the interview room next door. I'll bring him in.' De Vries got up and left the room.

Elly and I looked at each other. My head was hurting, but I wanted to talk to him. I had to talk to him. Soon de Vries returned with Tom Carson behind him. Tom looked pleased to see me. He was a much happier man than when I had last seen him.

'Miss Jensen,' he said, 'I'm so happy it's all over.' He smiled a big smile and sat down across the table from us.

'But why did you let Christiaans take over the club?' I asked. 'I don't understand.'

'I didn't have any choice,' said Carson. 'The club wasn't doing very well. We were very good in the late eighties, early nineties, then we started to go down. We lost some of our best players. We needed some money to buy new players, really good players. And to rebuild the stadium.'

I remembered that the stadium I had seen was new – and beautiful.

'We looked everywhere, but no-one wanted to put money into the club. Then Christiaans came along,'

Carson continued. 'He offered to put a lot of money into the club. But of course he wanted shares, ten per cent at first.'

Carson took a deep breath. 'The club is my whole life,' he said. 'I started it twenty years ago, a few years after I stopped playing. It was my dream, you know, to have a club and a school ... to really put something back into Dutch football. I couldn't let Rotterdam City Football Club just die. I love it too much.'

Tom Carson took another deep breath.

'So,' he continued, 'everything was fine at first. But soon Christiaans started asking for more,' he said. 'And then things started happening ... but for a long time I didn't know exactly what Christiaans was doing.'

'When did you find out about the Amsterdam Connection?' I asked.

'About a year ago,' he said. 'But by then Christiaans had forty-five per cent of the club and he was in a strong position. He said if I went to the police he would tell them I had been part of the syndicate too. Christiaans said the police would never believe I knew nothing about it. And I thought Max would think of something ... He always thought of something.'

Tom Carson smiled sadly. Christiaans had been too strong, even for Max.

'And well ... you know the rest,' said Tom. 'Max thought we should tell the police, but I wasn't sure. We argued about it. I didn't want to go to the police because I knew how dangerous Christiaans was. I was frightened for myself and the players.'

'And what are you going to do now?' I asked.

'Get back to the club and try to really make it work.' He smiled.

I shook Tom's hand. 'Good luck, Tom,' I said. 'I'm sure you'll do it.'

I was tired. I got up to leave.

'Miss Jensen,' said de Vries, smiling at last and holding out his hand. 'Thank you.'

I smiled back. The inspector was not an easy man, but he knew that he'd been wrong. I smiled at de Vries, but I didn't feel very happy. I had wanted to give him the evidence, to show him that I had been right, but now that I was here it didn't seem so important. I could only think about Max and Jos; they were dead and nothing would bring them back.

Chapter 16 *Goodbye Amsterdam*

I opened the door of de Vries's office. I had been awake all night and I was beginning to feel it. Elly followed me out.

'Are you going back to the hotel?' she asked.

'Yes,' I said. 'I've got a story to write if I still want my job in London.' I smiled at her and added, 'Oh, and Elly, thanks for everything. You've been a real friend.'

She put her arms around me. 'Yeah, thank you too, Kate,' said Elly. 'And Kate . . . '

'Mmm?'

'Don't come back to Amsterdam for a while, eh? I don't think I can take it.' She laughed.

I kissed Elly and left the police station. I walked back to the hotel through the city's empty streets. They were safe for me now that Christiaans was in a police cell. The salt smell of the sea cleared my head and the morning light danced on the water of the canals. Amsterdam was beautiful once more.

As I walked back I thought about the people I was leaving behind in Amsterdam: Elly, who had put herself in so much danger to help me; Raúl who had finally been brave enough to do what was right; my poor 'freind' Jos who had lost his life and Tom Carson who had lost his brother. I looked into the dark water of the canal and thought about Max. Max had saved my life all those years ago. He had fought for me when I needed it. And I had to fight for him when he couldn't fight for himself. Perhaps that was the meaning of friendship. Perhaps the only true one.

I wrote my story. An hour later, at 8.30 in the morning, it was finished. I faxed it through to the office back in London. It would be waiting for Balzano when he got into work.

I lay on my bed. I was exhausted and fell asleep. The phone woke me up. It was Balzano, shouting, but this time he was happy. 'Great story, Jensen!'

'Thanks,' I said. 'Oh, and Dave, I'd like to take two weeks off. I need a holiday.'

I held the telephone away from my ear and smiled. Some things never changed.

Cambridge English Readers

Other titles available at Level 4:

When Summer Comes
by Helen Naylor
Stephen and Anna Martins take a holiday break in a seaside village. There they make a new friend. But when Stephen is suddenly called back to London on business, their lives start to change.

Lady in White
by Colin Campbell
John is a successful TV producer with a happy family life. While researching a new programme, he comes across a story about a ghostly hitch-hiker that is very close to things that have happened in his own life. John's concern for his family turns to worry, then to blind panic in this chilling tale.

Nothing but the Truth
by George Kershaw
Hu is a student at an international school in Bangkok. She has a problem with a teacher and doesn't know what to do. An adventure in a park, acting in a musical and the help of friends make Hu realise she must tell nothing but the truth.

A Matter of Chance

by David Hill

Paul Morris's happy life in Italy changes when his wife dies suddenly. He develops a relationship with Sandra, a friend at work. But soon Paul finds himself in a world of international crime.

The Fruitcake Special and other stories *by Frank Brennan*

Five stories about discovery – a perfume that attracts men, a book that shows people's thoughts, a remarkable change in a woman's life, the secret of high intelligence, and a way of making time stand still – make up this entertaining collection.

But Was it Murder?

by Jania Barrell

Alex Forley had everything: good looks, money, a beautiful house, an attractive girlfriend and a close group of friends. But now he is dead. Was it murder? And if so, who was the murderer?

Other Titles by Sue Leather:

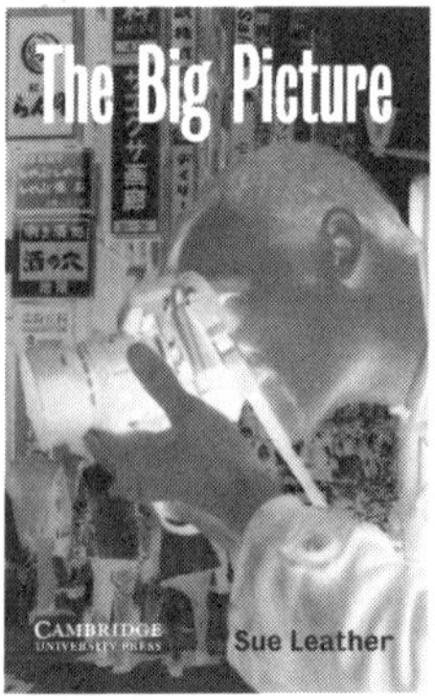

The Big Picture (Level 1)

Tokyo. Ken Harada takes photos for newspapers. But life gets dangerous when Ken takes a photo of a sumo star. Someone wants the photo badly. But who? And why?

Death in the Dojo (Level 5)

Reporter Kate Jensen is investigating the death of a karate master in a 'dojo', a karate training room, in London. Another death quickly follows and Jensen finds herself drawn into a mystery that leads her to Japan, and to a crime committed thirty years before.

Just Like a Movie (Level 1)

Brad Black goes to the movies every weekend with his girlfriend, Gina. They are happy, but they have no money. Then Brad has an idea and thinks that real life can be just like the movies – but that's when things go wrong.